Usborne

Starting Gardening

Sue Johnson and Cheryl Evans

Sue Johnson is Education Officer for the Royal Horticultural Society

Designed by Non Figg

Illustrated by Teri Gower

Photographs by Howard Allman

Contents

Before you start

Internet link: go to www.usborne-quicklinks.com for a link to a Web site where you can find lots of tips to get you started in the garden.

Gardening is interesting all year round. There is always something new to look at and things to plan and do.

A big garden takes a lot of caring for, but you can enjoy growing things in just a very small patch. In fact, you can grow most of the plants for the projects in this book in pots.

Gardening tools

Gardening is easier if you have a few tools to help you. You don't need to buy them all at once and you may be able to borrow some from parents or friends. It tells you at the start of each project in this book which tools you need.

You need a watering can you can lift when it is full. You can buy a small children's one.

Any watering can must have a special top on its spout, called a rose. This has small holes to make the water sprinkle instead of pour out.

You should wear gloves when touching soil.

You can buy a plastic sheet with handles for collecting garden waste, but plastic bags will do.

Scissors are handy.

Label what you plant by writing its name on plastic markers.

Trowel

Small fork

To work in a garden you need a rake to break up big lumps of earth.

Outdoors, a broom is useful to sweep up leaves and earth from paths.

A dibber makes holes in soil for planting seeds. A pencil or stick will do instead.

Plant pots

There are two main kinds of pots, plastic and terracotta (hard-baked clay). Terracotta pots are pretty, but heavy and break if dropped. Plastic pots are light and break less easily.

Pots are heavy when filled with soil. Put them where you want them before filling.

You need big pots for big plants.

You need string for many garden jobs. You can buy green garden string.

Earth in terracotta pots dries out more quickly than in plastic ones, so needs more watering.

Pots need one or more holes in the bottom to let water drain out. Plants don't like soggy soil.

Soil

In this book, when it says to use compost, use general purpose potting compost. You can buy this from garden centres. It is good soil with no pests or diseases in it. Don't just use soil from the garden.

Keeping safe

Here are some things you should be careful of in the garden.

• Don't try to lift things that are too heavy. Ask for help.

• Don't leave tools lying about or throw them around.

• Flowers make some people sneeze. This is called hayfever. If you suffer, it's better to grow plants without flowers.

• If you get a scratch, wash it thoroughly at once and cover it up. Dirt in cuts can make you ill.

• Keep your eyes open for dog or cat dirt in the garden. Never touch it.

• When you've finished, wash your hands and scrub your nails with a brush. Don't suck fingers or bite your nails with dirty hands.

Finding out about seeds

One way of growing plants is from seeds. You can collect seeds from plants in a garden or you can buy them in packets from a garden centre. Look carefully at the back of the packet. It tells you all about the seeds.

It says when to plant the seeds.

Names

All plants have a Latin name. Many have a common name, too, which most people call them. In this book you will see both names, like this:

Columbine (*Aquilegia*)
Common name *(Latin name)*

Do the plants prefer sun or shade?

It tells you when the flowers bloom, or the fruit ripen.

SOW BY 55
SEASON 1997
PKT YEAR END 31.5.97

HELICHRYSUM
Strawflower

Ideal for limited space.
Excellent for cutting
and drying.

QUICK GUIDE
Sow late winter to mid spring.
Flowers late summer to autumn.

INSTRUCTIONS FOR SOWING
Sow late winter to mid spring. Sow seed on surface of soil. Gently press down. Sealing in a plastic bag after sowing is helpful. Transplant when seedlings are big enough to handle. Grow on in cooler conditions. Let them get used to outdoor conditions for 10-15 days before planting out.
Plant out after all risk of frost is over. Plant 30cm (12in) apart in a sunny spot, in ordinary, well-drained soil.

It says how to sow the seeds on the packet, too.

The packet says what soil the seeds like (see page 30).

Kinds of plants

Some plants live longer than others. Look for these words on seed packets to tell you what kind of plant the seeds will become.

Hardy annuals. You plant the seeds in spring. They flower and die in one season.

Poppy (*Papaver*)

Half hardy annuals. Like *hardy annuals*, but need more care. You plant seeds indoors and only put them outside when you are sure there will be no more frost.

Petunia

Hardy biennials. You plant seeds in summer. They grow leaves in the first season but no flowers until the next year.

Sweet William (*Dianthus barbatus*)

Hardy perennials. The seeds may be planted in spring or autumn. They live for years and flower again and again. Their leaves and stems may die down in winter.

Columbine (*Aquilegia*)

Plants make seeds when the flowers die. Seeds fall on the soil and some grow into new plants the next year, except for *half hardy annuals* (see pages 6-7).

Internet link: go to *www.usborne-quicklinks.com* for a link to a Web site where you can find out how to make a shoebox greenhouse.

Seeds in the kitchen

When a seed gets wet, it sucks in water, swells and splits. It sends roots out into the soil and pushes shoots up. This is how it starts to grow into a plant.

Some of the things we eat are seeds. You can make them swell and sprout shoots and then eat them in a crunchy salad.

Brown lentils

Mung beans

Whole red lentils

You will need: seeds (see left - ones from wholefood shops work best); glass jars, one for each type of seed; thin fabric, such as cotton or muslin; tepid (which means slightly warm) water; rubber bands.

Chick peas

Chick peas in jar

Red lentil sprouts

Chick pea sprouts

Brown lentil sprouts

About two tablespoons of water

Put a handful of seeds in a jar. Pour in water to more than cover the seeds.

Stretch a piece of fabric over the jar. Hold it on with a rubber band.

Leave the jar overnight, then pour the water out through the fabric.

Drain gently so as not to snap shoots.

Next day, pour in more tepid water, shake gently but well, and drain again.

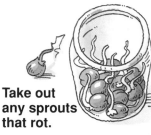

Take out any sprouts that rot.

Do this for three or four days. Can you see the seeds swell and start to sprout?

After about five days, tip the sprouts out and eat on a salad.

Sprouts may grow faster or slower - it depends on warmth and light.

Mung bean sprouts

5

Summer seedlings

Many pretty garden flowers are *half hardy annuals* (see page 4). To grow these, start the seeds off indoors. When they have grown into small plants, called seedlings, you can move them outside.

You will need: a seed tray with holes in the bottom; compost; flower seeds, such as Strawflower (*Helichrysum*), Stocks (*Matthiola*), Scabious (*Scabiosa*);trowel; dibber or stick; watering can; plastic food wrap; several 7cm (3in) pots, two or three 15cm (6in)pots.

Seedlings in seed tray.

Make a hole for bigger seeds with a finger.

You scatter tiny seeds.

Shoots take about a week.

Use the rose on the spout and water gently.

See if the compost is dry every few days.

1. Fill the seed tray with compost to 2cm (1in) below the rim. Sow the seeds as it says on the packet.

2. Scatter compost on top. Stretch food wrap over the tray. Keep it inside in a light place until shoots appear.

3. Take off the foodwrap as soon as shoots grow. Water the tray if the compost feels dry when you press the top.

Hold onto the lower leaves as you lift.

Never touch the roots.

Press gently around the stem to firm.

4. The first two leaves are the seed leaves. The next two are called true leaves. Now you can move them.

5. Half fill the small pots with compost. Push a stick into the soil by a seedling and lift up its roots and soil.

6. Hold the seedling in a pot. Fill in around it with compost. Do the same for each seedling. Keep inside.

There must be no more frost.

Tap the bottom of the pot.

7. Once the weather is warm, partly fill the 15cm (6in) pots with compost, as shown here.

8. Put a finger on either side of the seedling stem. Turn its pot over and tip seedling and compost out.

9. Hold the plant around its stem and put it in the big pot. Fill compost in around it. Press to hold it firm.

Internet link: go to **www.usborne-quicklinks.com** for a link to a Web site where you can learn how to make compost.

More blooms

If you pick the dead flowers off *half hardy annuals* all summer, they keep making new flowers.

Gently pinch dead flowers off stems.

This means there are no seeds left in autumn to make new plants, so you have to buy and sow more seeds each year.

These seedlings have been potted on into 7cm (3in) pots.

The yellow and orange flowers are Strawflowers (*Helichrysum*)

Brompton Stocks (*Matthiola*)

Seed tray

Flowers like these are especially good to pick for a bouquet or to put in a vase.

7

Bulbs

Some plants grow from bulbs. A bulb has layers of tightly packed leaves inside, like an onion, which is a bulb. It stores food for the plant. If you give it warmth and water, the bulb starts to come to life.

Outdoor pots

Bulbs are some of the first plants to flower outdoors in spring. Plant them outdoors in the early autumn in a pot, then be patient, it's worth the wait.

You will need:
a large plastic or terracotta pot with drainage holes - it must be frost-proof; compost to fill the pot; a stick; one or more sorts of bulbs, such as *Narcissus*, Dutch Crocus, Tulips.

Use the stick.
Put compost in the pot up to three-quarters full. Make a hole for a bulb.

Bulbs should not touch.

Rest the fat end of the bulb in the hole. Do the same for all the bulbs.

Top the pot up with compost. Cover the bulbs completely. Put the pot outside.

Don't leave pots out in bad frosts.

Narcissi

Ivy

You don't need to water pots outside.

When leaf tips first appear you know your bulbs are growing.

Primula

Crocus

Layers inside bulb

Winter pansy

Plant winter flowers in the pot to liven it up until bulbs flower.

Bulb tips

Bury bulbs in the ground as deep as their own length.

Plant some bulbs to bloom together and some to bloom at different times for a longer display.

The package says when they bloom.

In pots, let the flowers and leaves die. Then dig out the bulbs to save until next year. Leave bulbs in the garden where they are.

Bulbs indoors

Plant bulbs in a pot indoors in the same way as for outdoors. Leave the tips of larger bulbs showing above the compost. Put them in a cool, dark place indoors for eight to ten weeks. Then move to a light, cool spot.

◀ **The roots grow first in the cool and dark. Leaves and flowers grow in the light.** ▶

Narcissus **called Paper Whites are specially for growing indoors.**

Only put indoor bulbs in a warm room once flower buds appear.

Winter hyacinths

Not many flowers bloom in the middle of winter, but some bulbs are specially treated to do so indoors. Hyacinths don't even need soil if you grow them like this.

You will need: old gloves (the treated bulb may irritate bare skin); a treated hyacinth bulb; a glass jar; three toothpicks.

Wear gloves to do this.

Nearly fill the jar with cold water. Push toothpicks into the fattest part of the bulb.

Bulb should sit about ½cm (¼in) above the water.

Rest the toothpicks on the rim of the jar so the fat end of the bulb is near the water.

Watch the roots appear first, then the leaves. It will be about 15 weeks before the flower blooms.

You can buy a shaped Hyacinth jar like this. Then you don't need toothpicks.

Don't add more water. The roots reach down to it.

Once the roots have grown, move to a cool, light place.

Leave the jar in a cool, dark place out of the frost. A shed or garage is good.

9

Houseplant cuttings

Plants grown in pots indoors are called houseplants. You can buy many pretty ones, but you can also take a piece off a healthy plant to grow a new one. This is called taking cuttings and you can see some different ways to do it here. Ask friends if they have plants which you could take cuttings from.

Take several cuttings at once. They may not all work.

African violet (Saintpaulia) and three leaf cuttings

Leaf cuttings

One way to grow new plants is from the leaf of a big plant. Here's one way to do this.

> **You will need:** 7cm (3in) pot and compost; sharp scissors; stick; a plant such as African violet (Saintpaulia), Peperomia or Begonia (there are lots of different kinds of Begonia).

Lean against edge of pot.

Make a clean snip. Don't crush stem.

Snip off a large, fully-grown leaf with about 5cm (2in) of stem. Push the stem into the pot of compost as shown.

New leaves should form at the base of the leaf after about three or four weeks. New roots will have grown.

Be careful not to break the roots.

Gently lift the plantlet out. Replant it in a fresh pot of soil (see page 6 for how to re-pot small plants).

Runners

Parent

Plantlets

Runner – cut this when new roots have grown.

Spider plant (Chlorophytum)

Some house plants grow new plants, or plantlets, at the end of long stems called runners. Plant these in their own pot.

Geranium
(*Pelargonium*)
cutting in jar

Begonia plant
with cuttings

Spider plant
(*Chlorophytum*)
with plantlets

Stem cuttings

If you cut a stem off some plants and put it in compost or water it will grow roots and start a new plant.

You will need: a small pot with compost OR a glass jar of water; a healthy plant, such as a Busy Lizzie *(Impatiens)* or Geranium *(Pelargonium)*.

Main stem
Side branch

1. Gently pull a side branch off a main stem. Pick one that has new shoots growing on it if you can.

2. Poke a hole in the compost with a finger. Place the stem in the hole and firm it in.

Use a dibber
or stick.

Water if the compost feels dry.

3. In about three or four weeks, the cutting should make new leaves and start to grow.

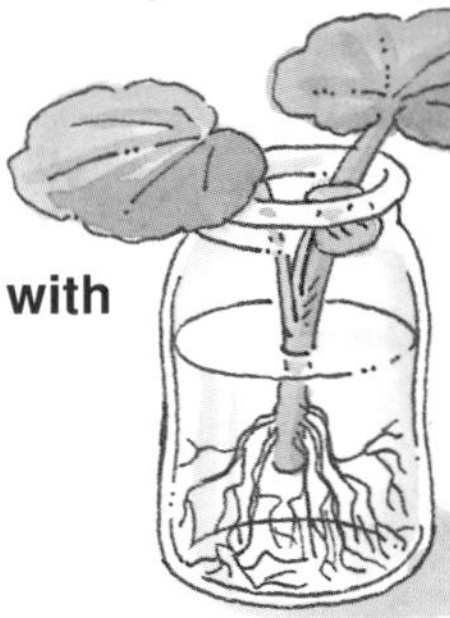

Try this method with another cutting.

See which method works best.

4. Instead of using compost, you could stand a stem cutting in a jar of water. See if roots grow.

5. When the roots are well grown, poke a hole in the compost big enough for them and plant the cutting.

Grow a salad

Internet link: go to *www.usborne-quicklinks.com* for a link to a Web site with photos of gardens full of things you can eat.

Eating things you grow is one of the best parts of gardening. Here are some things that are easy to grow and tasty to eat. Plant them in late spring or early summer (check the packets).

You will need: seeds for some of these: mixed leaves lettuce; radishes, spring onions; a large window box; compost; stones or broken pieces of terracotta pot; plant labels.

Stones stop holes from getting clogged so water drains out better.

Plant each kind of seed in one patch. Mark them with labels.

Keep the seed packets.

1. Put stones or broken terracotta pots in the bottom of a window box. Then fill the box with compost.

2. Scatter seeds thinly on the top - you can plant several kinds. Then cover with a thin layer of compost.

Water often if it is hot and dry.

They taste best when young.

3. Put the box outside in a light place, but not in direct sunlight. Water the plants if they don't get any rain.

4. As they grow, pull out plants that are smaller and weaker than the rest to give the strongest ones room.

5. They should be ready to eat in about six weeks. Check the seed packet for when's best to pick them.

Lettuce seeds

Lettuce seedling

Grown lettuce leaf

Radish seeds

Chopped radish

Grown radish

Radish seedling

Chopped spring onions

Young spring onion

Spring onion seedling

Spring onion seeds

Tomatoes

Tomatoes are *half hardy annuals* (see page 4) so you have to sow seeds inside or in a greenhouse, as shown on pages 6-7. Plant them out when there is no more frost.

You will need: tomato plant seedlings: try Sweet 100, or Tigerella; special tomato compost - from garden stores; a large pot; a garden cane about 75cm (30in long); garden string.

1. Fill the pot with soil. With a trowel, dig a hole in the middle big enough for the tomato seedling's roots.

Gently press soil around the stem to hold firm.

Don't tie it too tight or you'll cut the stem.

2. Plant the seedling in the hole. Push the cane in near the stem. Tie the stem to the cane gently with string.

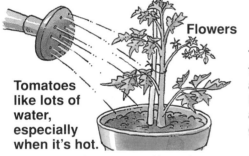

Flowers

Tomatoes like lots of water, especially when it's hot.

3. Water the pot well and put it in a sunny place outside. Water it every day as the plant grows and flowers.

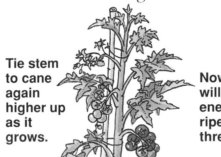

Tie stem to cane again higher up as it grows.

4. If you are lucky, each flower will form a tomato. Each bunch of tomatoes is called a truss.

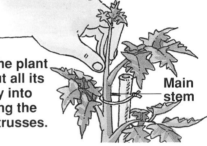

Now the plant will put all its energy into ripening the three trusses.

Main stem

5. Once the plant has three trusses, pinch off the top of the main stem between a finger and thumb.

Tomatoes will even turn red after they are picked if you put them somewhere warm.

6. The tomatoes swell and grow fat. With plenty of warmth they turn red. Then they are ready to pick.

You could add some bean sprouts (page 5).

You can make a delicious salad you have grown yourself.

Herbs

Herbs are plants whose leaves have a tangy taste and smell. People have used them to add zest to food since ancient times.

You can grow many herbs from seeds, but these pages show you how to take cuttings from herb plants. Ask someone in your family, or a friend, if you can take cuttings from their herbs.

Herb knot garden

Because they are so varied, you can make patterns with herbs. A herb garden with a formal pattern is called a knot garden.

You will need: a large pot with drainage holes; a bowl about 15cm (6in) across; about 10 cuttings each of three different herbs, such as Rosemary, Lavender (take cuttings as for Rosemary on page 15), Thyme (take cuttings as for Marjoram on page 15), Sage, Savory; compost.

This pot has three circles with a "knot" of all three herbs in the middle.

Make circles touch edge of pot and overlap in the middle.

1. Put stones in the pot then fill it up with compost. Mark three overlapping circles with the bowl rim.

2. Pull the lower leaves off the stems of one herb. Push the stems into the compost around one marked circle.

Once roots form, these herbs will grow to different sizes. Replant them in pots or the garden.

3. Do the same with a second herb around another circle.

4. Repeat with the third herb around the last circle. They overlap in the middle.

Drink mint tea really cold with ice.

Herb cubes

Mint tea

Make tea and pour it into a jug. Add sugar and lots of chopped mint and leave to cool. Keep in a refrigerator.

Herb cubes

Put chopped herbs and water in an ice tray. Freeze, then store in a plastic bag. Add to stews and soups.

Internet link: *go to* **www.usborne-quicklinks.com** *for a link to a Web site where you can learn how to grow, dry and store different kinds of herbs.*

To dry herbs, tie in small bunches (all the same kind) and hang in an airy place for two to three weeks.

Rub leaves between your hands to crumble.

Store dried herbs in a clean jar with a lid.

Lavender is not to eat, but smells lovely.

Thyme   Mint

Mint

(Mentha)

Mint grows and spreads really quickly. It's best to keep it in a pot of its own so it does not overcrowd other herbs.

Cut a stem of mint, put it in water and keep it somewhere light but not in direct sun. Watch the roots grow, then plant into a pot of compost.

Marjoram

(Origanum vulgare)

In the spring, dig a trowel into a spreading marjoram plant. Cut all the way through the roots and dig up part of it with roots on. Plant in a pot of compost.

One kind of Marjoram is called Oregano. This is nice sprinkled on pizzas.

Rosemary is a shrub. Shrubs have woody stems.

Rosemary

(Rosmarinus officinalis)

Gently pull a side shoot down and off the main stem, peeling a sliver of the main stem with it. This is called a heel cutting. Plant it in compost.

Chives

(Allium schoenoprasum)

Dig up a clump of chives. You will find lots of little bulbs. Separate a few and plant them in compost. Firm the clump back into the soil as it was.

Kitchen surprises

There are lots of things in the kitchen which will grow if you plant them. Some of them make surprising plants.

You will need: pips from an orange, lemon, grapefruit or any other fruit; compost; small pots; clear plastic (from a plastic bag); rubber band.

Pick plump pips.

Plant the pip soon after taking it from the fruit.

Fruit left on the pip may rot and spoil it.

1. Wash and dry a pip. Fill a pot with compost. Push the pip 1cm (½in) into the compost.

2. If you try small pips (such as from grapes), push them only ½cm (¼in) into the compost.

3. Cover the pot with a piece of clear plastic. Hold this on around the rim with the rubber band.

This is a lemon plant. It takes a long time to grow this big.

Keep checking your seed pots. It's exciting when shoots start to grow.

Shoots should show in two to eight weeks. Take off the plastic then.

If it's hot, water more often.

4. Put the pot indoors in a light place but not in direct sunlight.

5. Feel the compost every day and water it when it feels dry (about once a week).

Lemons and grapefuits will grow outside in hot, sunny places. In cool places, you can put them outside in summer, but bring them in before it gets frosty.

Lemon pips growing

Grapefruit pip growing

These plants won't have fruit for many years.

Avocado plant

You can grow a lovely big plant from the stone inside an avocado. Ask if you can keep the stone when someone has bought an avocado to eat.

You will need: a stone from an avocado; container to soak it in; glass jar; three toothpicks; 10cm (4in) pot; compost.

1. Wash the seed. Put it in tepid water in a container and leave it somewhere warm for two days.

Round end

See the *Hyacinth* bulb on page 9 for how to do this.

2. Balance the stone on three toothpicks. It should touch the water.

Shoots may appear in as little as 10 days.

If there is no sign after five weeks, try another one.

Make a dip in the middle.

Only half cover the stone.

3. Leave it inside, somewhere warm and not too light. Keep the jar topped up with tepid water.

4. When the first shoot appears, it is ready to plant. Fill the pot with compost.

5. Make a dip to sit the stone in. Take care not to break any roots. Push compost in around it.

Ginger and garlic

Garlic is a bulb and ginger is a root. Separate a few cloves of garlic and push them into compost. Push a knobby ginger root into compost.

Ginger

Garlic

Garlic clove

Plant blunt end of garlic clove.

These garlic shoots smell garlicky.

This extraordinary shoot is from a ginger root.

Plant the ginger with the knobby bits pointing up.

Flowers of the mountains

Some plants grow in particular places. Where they live gives you a clue to what weather, soil and other conditions they like.

The snow never melts above this level.

Alpine plants grow between these two levels.

No trees grow above this level.

If you want to grow them, you must create a place as much like their natural home as possible. Alpine plants live on mountains.

Mountain soil is thin and gritty.

There's a lot of wind high up on mountain sides.

Alpine plants often grow in the shelter of rocks, out of the wind.

Watering

Give them more water in spring.

Water runs quickly off rocky mountain sides, so alpines don't like to stand in the wet. They don't like water on their flowers and leaves either, so only water the grit around the plants.

An alpine garden

Many alpine plants don't need a lot of special care if you give them the right conditions to start with.

You will need: 3 alpine plants in pots; a tray with holes (such as a big seed tray), a little deeper than the pots; sand; grit; a stone from the garden or waste ground. Don't take stones from walls or the country.

Where do they look best?

1. Choose three plants (see some on page 19). Place them, and the stone, in the tray and arrange them.

Pack the sand tightly around the pots.

2. Take out the stone. Leave the plants in their pots and fill in around them with sand. Put the stone back in.

Sprinkle grit right up to plant stems.

3. Spread a layer of grit on top of the sand and over the compost in the pots.

4. Place the tray outdoors where it is light, warm and airy, not in direct sunlight.

See how to water alpines above.

Don't let the pots dry out.

5. Poke your finger under the grit to see if the soil is dry. Water to keep it moist.

Plants to choose

Most alpine plants are small. They look especially nice together if you choose ones with different flowers and leaves. Pick some that are taller than others, too.

Sempervivum grow in rosettes of pointed leaves.

There are lots of different kinds of Saxifrage *(Saxifraga).*

Lewisia has pretty pink flowers.

Many *Campanula* species have delicate blue flowers.

Primula are bright and very varied.

Dianthus has narrow leaves and pink or white flowers.

Aubrieta trails over the edge of a pot.

In the tray above: a *Dianthus* (left), a Saxifrage (middle), a *Phlox* (right).

This is a small *Cyclamen.*

The spiky plant is a *Ranunculus.* The two like round cushions are Saxifrages.

Another idea

Plant small bulbs (see page 9) between your alpine plants in the autumn.

Mark where you plant bulbs

These blue flowers are Gentians.

You can move the plant pots easily.

Bulbs will add extra interest to your tray in the spring.

Look at the labels to make sure the bulbs only grow fairly small. Big flowers would swamp your delicate alpines. You may be able to get kinds called "dwarf", which are good.

Ferns

Ferns are found all over the world and there are many different kinds. Some kinds have been around since more than 350 million years ago. They can have many different leaf shapes and make a lovely green display planted together.

See how to start a fern garden like this on the page opposite.

If the glass steams up so you cannot see the ferns, it is too wet in the jar. Leave the top off for a while.

Put stones in to make a landscape. Don't use wood, as it rots.

You need to stand the fern bottle in a light place, but not in direct sunlight

Indoor ferns

There are different kinds of ferns to plant outdoors and indoors. Read the label to see where an outside fern likes to grow before you plant one. These are indoor ferns you could use in a bottle garden.

Mediterranean Brake (*Pteris cretica*)

Rabbit's foot fern (*Davallia species*

Bird's Nest Fern (*Asplenium nidus*)

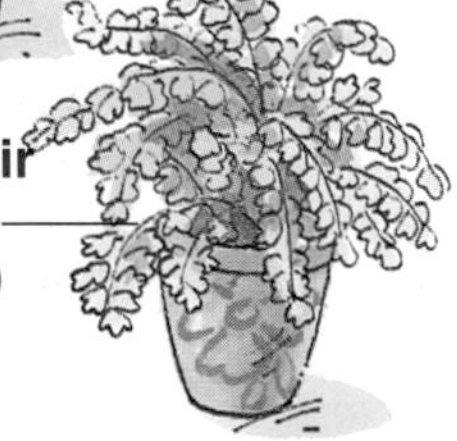

Venus Maidenhair Fern (*Adiantum capillus-veneris*)

Amazing curls

Some outdoor ferns lose their leaves in winter. Their leaves uncurl back to life in the spring as shown here.

Fern bottle garden

Here's an interesting way to plant some ferns indoors.

You will need: 2 or 3 ferns (choose small ones, as they grow quickly); multi-purpose compost; gravel; charcoal pieces (from aquarium stores); a large, clear glass or plastic jar with a wide lid; a large plastic drink bottle; scissors; an old spoon; strong tape; a garden cane about 30cm (12in) long; a water sprayer.

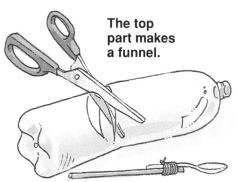

The top part makes a funnel.

Make the compost about 1-2cm (½ - 1in) deep.

1. Ask for help to cut the bottle around the middle. Tape the cane to the spoon to make a long handle.

2. Put a layer of gravel and charcoal in the bottom of the jar. This is to keep the compost well drained.

Funnel stops jar from getting dirty.

Tip the jar from side to side to get an even depth of compost.

Hold plant so that you can lower your hand into the jar.

3. Through the funnel, add enough compost to plant the fern roots in. It should come no higher than one third up the jar.

4. Dig a hole in the compost with the spoon. Lower a fern into it and firm it in with the spoon. Repeat with all the ferns.

5. If the compost isn't moist, spray it and the ferns with water. Spray any soil off the sides of the jar, too. Then put the lid on tightly.

Watering themselves

Your fern jar will rarely need water. The ferns water themselves, like this.

The fern sucks up water from the soil and takes in all it needs.

Any extra water escapes from tiny holes in the leaves as a gas called water vapour. This is called transpiration.

The water vapour touches the cold glass and water droplets form. This is called condensation.

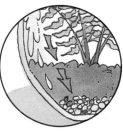

The drops roll back down into the compost and keep it moist.

21

Ivy shapes

You can see all kinds of ivy growing up walls and fences or hanging prettily over the lip of a window box or pot. Cuttings of green, silver, gold or curly ivies are easy to take and grow, like this.

Ways to climb

Climbing ivies have little roots growing off their stems, called aerial roots. These reach out and cling to whatever the ivy climbs up.

Sweet Peas have tendrils. They wrap around twiggy sticks that are put in to support them.

Honeysuckle stems twine around a support such as a cane or trellis.

Ivy cuttings

You will need: an ivy plant from which to take cuttings. (You can find ivy all over the place -as long as you only take a few cuttings you won't harm it.); small pots; compost; dibber or stick.

Now the cutting will have roots, too.

Old leaves should still look fresh.

2. In three to four weeks, there should be some new leaves.

Shoot

Pull off the lower leaves.

1. Pinch the top 7cm (3in) off the tip of a shoot. Push the stem into the compost.

Dig cutting out gently.

3. Lift the ivy gently with a stick and plant it where you want it to grow.

This is an ivy topiary in a fun shape (see page 23).

Wind the ivy around the wire if it starts growing the wrong way.

The more you trim your topiary, the bushier it will become.

Ivy topiary

Training a plant to grow in a special shape is called topiary. You can do topiary with ivy. It has lots of leaves and twining stems that can be trained around a shape.

You will need: 2 or 3 ivy cuttings with roots - try *Hedera helix* cultivars (there are lots of different kinds); strong garden wire; large pot; compost; pliers.

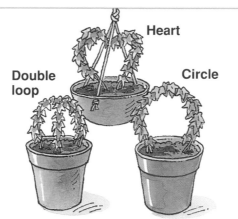

Double loop

Heart

Circle

1. Fill the pot with compost. Decide what shape to make. Here are some simple ideas.

Cut with pliers if needed. Ask an adult to help.

Bind tape around ends to keep together and avoid sharp points.

2. Twist together three or four lengths of garden wire. Bend this into the shape you want the ivy trained around.

3. Push wire ends well into the compost. Add more wire until you have completed the shape.

4. Plant an ivy cutting at each end of each wire. If it's long enough, twist the ivy stem around the wire.

5. As the ivy grows, tie the stems to the wire shapes to keep them tidy, if you need to.

Plant a cutting at each end of each wire shape.

Use cuttings from different kinds of ivy to make it more interesting.

Topiary serpent

This ivy topiary serpent is simple to make. Put separate wire shapes in a window box, as shown.

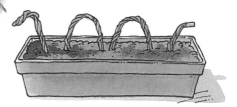

Plant ivy cuttings as in the steps above and trim the ivy to keep the shape neat.

23

A garden for wildlife

There are millions of tiny creatures in every trowelful of soil. Lots of other insects, birds and animals may also visit a garden.

Some harm plants but many others help the garden stay healthy. You can grow plants in your garden to encourage helpful wildlife.

Flowers for wildlife

These are some of the flowers that help attract wildlife into a garden. The more variety there is, the better, but even just a few will begin to attract more insects. When there are more insects in the garden, the other animals will follow to eat them.

Garden friends

Here are some of the ways wildlife helps a garden.

If there are lots of insects flying at night, bats may come to eat them.

Hoverfly

Bees, butterflies, moths and some flies help flowers make their seeds or fruit (see how on page 27).

Ladybirds and hoverflies have young called larvae. These eat bugs called aphids, which suck sap from plants.

Hedgehogs and toads eat slugs, which eat plants and damage them.

Ladybird

Ground beetles and spiders like to live in long grass.

Birds eat lots of insects that harm plants.

Plants cannot live in soggy soil with no air in it. Worms wriggle through the soil and leave air holes that water can drain away through.

Ground beetles eat many pests in the soil, such as weevils, which eat plant roots.

Sunflowers

Sunflowers and any plants with berries attract birds. See how to plant a Sunflower on page 26.

Californian poppy

Try Californian Poppy and Pot Marigolds to appeal to hoverflies.

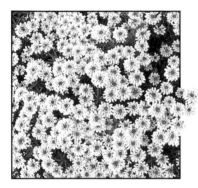

Candytuft

Plant Candytuft, Sedum and Buddleia for butterflies.

Evening Primrose

For moths, try flowers that bloom or smell at night, such as Evening Primrose or Honeysuckle.

Snapdragon

Plant flowers such as Snapdragon, Marjoram or Lavender for lots of bees.

Garden quiz

When you visit a garden, look for things that wildlife would like. Look at the garden in this picture and see if you can answer the questions below.

Honeysuckle

Herb garden

Holly bush

1. Where could birds shelter and build nests safely?
2. Where might spiders and ground beetles live?
3. Which parts would bees like best?
4. Where could a hedgehog hide?
5. What wildlife might like the pond?
6. What might eat the berries on the holly bush in winter?
7. Where could a bird have a drink or a wash?
8. Which part of the garden do the butterflies like best? Do you know why?

(Answers on page 32.)

25

Sunflower

Plant a Sunflower in spring and watch it grow - it could grow much taller than you. See if it attracts bees and butterflies. Then, in autumn, its round head is full of seeds which birds will eat. Plant it in a sunny spot in the garden, or in a pot on a balcony or patio.

You will need: Sunflower seeds; small pots, large pots and compost if you are growing them in pots; tall stick or cane; garden string.

Sunflowers are less likely to be knocked down by the wind here.

1. In a garden, push three or four seeds no more than 2.5cm (1in) into the soil. Put them next to a wall or fence if you can, for shelter.

Fully grown Sunflower

Use the small pots.

Wait until the true leaves (the second set) grow.

2. You can either plant just one seed in a pot, or put two or three in. Plant a single seedling on into a big pot as on page 6.

3. If you plant a few seeds and they all grow, carefully tip them out with the compost. Gently pull them apart and pot each one.

If all the seeds grow in the garden, take out any weak ones. If you want a very tall Sunflower, take out all but the strongest one.

Watch it turn its head to follow the sun.

Make sure you water your Sunflowers a lot.

Tie string tightly to cane, then loosely around the stem.

½cm (¼in) gap

Sunflower seedlings

4. To support the sunflower as it grows taller, push a stick or cane in beside the stem. Tie the stem to the stick with garden string.

5. Sunflowers grow very tall. Tie the stem to the cane again higher up as it grows. You may need to put in a longer cane.

Strawberries

Internet link: go to www.usborne-quicklinks.com for links to a Web site with a movie about pollination and a site with a strawberry smoothie recipe.

If you like strawberries, try growing Wood or Alpine Strawberries, which grow from seeds. Sow seeds in spring in the garden or in a pot outside. If you buy or borrow a cold frame (see right), you can sow even before it's really warm and give them a head start.

Using a cold frame

You keep a cold frame outside.

Glass or plastic lid.

Open lid on warm days and close at night.

A cold frame is a wooden box with a clear lid. You put seeds in pots inside it.

The sides protect the plant from frost. The air inside warms up under the sun.

Making fruit

All fruit plants need bees to help them make fruit. A bee visits Strawberry flowers to collect the honey-like nectar inside, which is its food. Its furry body also collects a powder, called pollen, from the flowers.

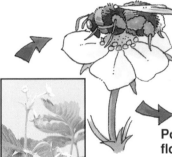

Pollen on its body from one flower rubs off on the next one. This is called pollination.

Pollinated flowers begin to form strawberries. The flower petals fall off to show a tiny strawberry in the middle.

The strawberry grows bigger. It is green, then it goes red as it ripens.

Spreading fruit

The big strawberries you buy in shops grow on plants with runners, like the Spider Plant (page 10). One plant spreads over a whole patch in time.

This is an Alpine Strawberry. It has small, sweet fruit.

Drying flowers

You can keep and enjoy flowers you grow by drying them. Whatever flower heads you want to dry, try to pick them just before they are fully open. Don't wait until they have been wide open for a few days.

You will need: permission to pick some flowers from your or a friend's garden. Try Poppies (*Papaver orientale*), Lavender (*Lavendula*),Strawflowers (*Helichrysum*), Cotton Lavender (*Santolina*), Love-in-a-mist (*Nigella*); a rubber band for each type of flower; string; scissors.

Statice (*Limonium*)

This spiky Sea Thistle (*Eryngium*) makes pretty shapes.

Strawflowers (*Helichrysum*) stay bright when dried.

Lavender has a strong, delicious scent.

Dry poppy seed heads

Pick long stems.

1. Pick the flowers on a dry day, late in the morning, so the sun has dried any dew on the flowers.

The rubber band tightens as the stems dry.

2. Pull the lower leaves off the stems. Hold the stems together and put a rubber band around them tightly.

Check and take out rotting flowers.

Keep different flowers in separate bunches.

3. Fan the flower heads out so they don't touch. Parts that touch will not dry well, and may rot.

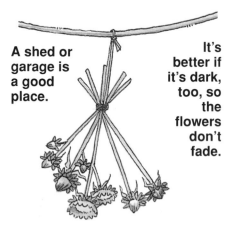

A shed or garage is a good place.

It's better if it's dark, too, so the flowers don't fade.

4. Push string or a hook of wire under the rubber band. Tie or hook the bunch onto a line in a cool, airy place.

*Internet link: go to **www.usborne-quicklinks.com** for a link to a Web site with lots of flower e-cards to send to friends and family.*

Pressing flowers

Many flowers will stay bright when you press them and look very pretty. Flat flowers, such as pansies, are easiest to press. It's hard to press really juicy flowers, such as hyacinths. Use pressed flowers for cards and gifts.

You will need:
permission to pick some flowers to press; try Pansies, Violets, Primroses, Poppies, Daisies, Buttercups; newspapers or blotting paper; a few heavy books.

Pressed *Fuchsias*

Cards made with pressed flowers.

1. Pick the flowers when they are newly opened and dry (not wet with rain or dew).

Don't let flowers touch.

2. Put paper on one side of an open book. Lay flowers on top. Press the middles very gently to flatten them.

Primula

Fuchsia

Lay the paper down gradually, pressing with your other hand as you go.

3. Place more paper on top. Try to make sure the flowers are flat. Close the other side of the book.

4. Put several more heavy books on top. Leave them for about two weeks to dry and flatten.

You can buy a flower press. You put flowers between its layers of cardboard and blotting paper.

Bolts at the corners screw down and press the layers tightly.

Primula

Nasturtium

Internet link: go to www.usborne-quicklinks.com for a link to a Web site where you can learn how to make picture frames for your dried flowers.

More gardening basics

Internet link: go to **www.usborne-quicklinks.com** *for a link to a Web site where you can learn how to make a scarecrow.*

Types of soil

There are many different types of soil. Plants grow better in some than others and different plants prefer different soils. It takes an expert to tell exactly what kind of soil you have, but here is a rough guide. Pick up a handful of moist garden soil and feel it.

Clay is made of tightly-packed particles.

Water drains very slowly through it.

It can get waterlogged.

Sandy soil is made of bigger particles.

Water drains through and it can dry out easily.

If you can roll the soil into a sausage shape, it probably has lots of clay in it. If you cannot make a sausage and it feels gritty, it is probably sandy soil.

Most soils can be improved by mixing in compost. It helps to open up clayey soils, to hold water in sandy soils and to add plant food to poor soils.

Garden design

Gardens look very different depending on what is grown in them and how they are laid out; their design, in other words.

Flower and leaf shapes and sizes and how they are mixed together give very different effects. You can even design a pot of plants.

Interesting leaves add variety.

Mix tall, slim flowers and shorter, flatter plants.

Blue, white and mauve flowers look cool.

Plant shorter flowers in front of tall ones.

Trailing plants add more variety and soften the edges of the pot.

Red, yellow and orange flowers look hot.

Weeds

Weeds are plants that you don't want growing in your garden. They take water and nutrients (food for plants) from the soil so there are less for your plants. Some grow very big, or spread and take over the garden. An experienced gardener can help you recognize weeds at first.

Weeds should be pulled out regularly.

A strange leaf among leaves you know may be a weed.

Glossary

Some of the gardening words used in this book are explained here. There are also some others that are not used in the book.

Alpines Plants that grow between tree level and snow level on mountains (pages 18-19).

Annual Plants that make flowers and die in one season (page 4).

Biennial Plants that grow leaves in their first season, but don't flower until their second year.

Bulb Tightly packed layers of leaves. Store of food for the leaves and flowers of *Hyacinth* and *Narcissus*, for example.

Compost heap Place in the garden where you pile dead flowers and leaves. These rot into a compost that is good for the garden.

Corm Store of food in a short, swollen stem, for plants such as *Crocus*. Corms are solid, not in layers like bulbs.

Cuttings Leaves or stems taken from a growing plant to start a new one.

Dead-heading Pinching dead flowers from plants. Many plants will make more flowers afterwards (page 7).

Dibber Stick for making holes in soil, or for lifting seedlings out of the soil.

Fertilizer Chemicals to put on the soil to make things grow better. They may be poisonous so should only be used carefully by adults.

Fork A big fork with a long handle is to dig the garden standing up; a small fork with a short handle is for digging in pots.

Frost When the temperature goes below freezing in winter, there is a frost. Pots outside can crack if they freeze, then warm up. Frost-proof pots should not crack.

Half-hardy Half-hardy plants die if they are out in a frost (see above). They must only be planted outside when there are no more frosts. They die with the first frosts of autumn.

Hardy Hardy plants can survive the frost. They may die down but they come back to life the next year.

Manure Animal (often horse) droppings. May be mixed with straw into the soil to make it good for growing plants.

Perennial Type of plant that goes on flowering for many years.

Plantlet New, small plant.

Pollination When bees carry pollen from flower to flower. This helps the flower to grow fruit (see page 27).

Potting on Moving a plant to a bigger pot so it has room to grow.

Roots These grow into the soil to hold the plant firm, and suck in water and other chemicals the plant needs.

Runners Long stems from some plants (pages 10,27). Plantlets grow on them.

Seed Part of a flowering plant that forms when the flower dies; you grow new plants from seeds. See pages 4-7.

Seedling Tiny plant when it first grows from a seed.

Shoots New growth on a plant or first growth above the soil.

Shrub Plant with woody stems and branches, such as Rosemary.

Terracotta Italian word meaning baked clay. Many flower pots are made of it.

Topiary Training plants into a special shape (see pages 22-23).

Trowel Small, short spade for digging up small plants, or digging in pots.

Truss One bunch of fruit on a branch (see page 13).

Index

Answers from page 25

1. Birds might nest in the trees, in plants that climb up walls or fences, or in the nesting box on the trellis at the back.
2. Beetles and spiders might live in the long grass under the trees, in gaps in the brick wall and the log pile.
3. Bees love the herb garden and flower beds.

4. A hedgehog would hide under plants and hedges.
5. Insects like ponds, and maybe frogs or toads, too.
6. Birds would eat the holly berries.
7. In the birdbath, or at the edge of the pond.
8. They like the flowers on the left side. Purple, blue and yellow flowers attract them most.

Acknowledgements
With thanks to:

Madee Broome, RHS, for expert advice;
Architectural Plants, Exotic Plants for London Gardens, Horsham, Sussex, for the loan of plants;
Capital Gardens plc, Alexandra Palace, London, for the loan of gardening equipment;
Rachael Swan for research;
Janet Johnson for the cover photograph.
Library photographs from Colgrave Seeds Ltd., West Adderbury, Banbury, Oxfordshire.